curious about

DISNEY

BY RACHEL GRACK

AMICUS

What are you

curious about?

CHAPTER THREE

Bet You Didn't Know ...

PAGE

16

Curious About is published by Amicus
P.O. Box 227
Mankato, MN 56002
www.amicuspublishing.us

Editor: Alissa Thielges
Series and Book Designer: Kathleen Petelinsek
Cover Designer: Lori Bye
Photo Researcher: Omay Ayres

Library of Congress Cataloging-in-Publication Data
Names: Koestler-Grack, Rachel A., 1973- author.
Title: Curious about disney / Rachel Grack.
Description: Mankato, MN: Amicus, [2024] | Series: Curious about favorite brands | Includes bibliographical references and index. | Audience: Ages 6–9 | Audience: Grades 2–3 | Summary: "Nine kid-friendly questions take elementary readers behind the scenes of Disney to spark their curiosity about the brand's history and products. A Stay Curious! feature modelsresearch skills while simple infographics support visual literacy"—Provided by publisher.
Identifiers: LCCN 2022032141 (print) | LCCN 2022032142 (ebook) | ISBN 9781645493266 (library binding) | ISBN 9781681528502 (paperback) | ISBN 9781645494140 (ebook)
Classification: LCC TL236.2 .K638 2024 (print) | LCC TL236.2 (ebook) | DDC 629.228/5—dc23
LC record available at https://lccn.loc.gov/2022032141
LC ebook record available at https://lccn.loc.gov/2022032142

Photos © Alamy/Album, 17, Pictorial Press Ltd 5, 9 (*Snow White, Mary Poppins*), 11 (4, 6), 19, United Archives GmbH 9 (Jungle Book); Dreamstime/Enchanted _fairy 9 (*Frozen II*), Flipcrab85 20–21, Mike Ricci 14 (top), Pindiyath100 12 (bottom), 15 (bottom), 18, Pv Productions 11 (bottom), Shaunwilkinson 15 (top left), Viavaltours 15 (top right), Wisconsinart 14 (bottom); Getty/Medios y Media cover, 1; Shutterstock/aijiro 11 (5), danmiami 6–7, Faiz Zaki 13 (bottom), Frame Stock Footage 11 (3), Morumotto 13 (top), Sarunyu L 12 (top), Tutatamafilm 11 (1), Willrow Hood 9 (*Toy Story*); Wikimedia Commons/Coolcaesar 11, Ed Bierman 11 (2), Walt Disney Productions 8, Winkler Pictures 4

Printed in China

Who started Disney?

Two brothers, Walt and Roy. They had big dreams. Walt Disney was an artist. He drew cartoons. Roy was a businessman. In 1923, they **filmed** the "Alice Comedies" together. Alice was a real girl with a cartoon cat. These short movies used both live action and **animation**. They became the first cartoons by the Walt Disney Company.

Walt Disney (right) stands with his brother, Roy.

DID YOU KNOW?
Walt Disney sold his first drawing at age seven!

Does Disney do more than movies?

A Disney cruise sets sail from Miami, Florida.

Yes, a lot more! Disney is a huge **entertainment** company. It makes TV shows, books, toys, and games. Disney owns **theme parks** and cruise ships. It is one of the biggest **brands** in the world. But Disney is more than just a business. Its goal is to make people happy. And it has been doing that for 100 years!

CHAPTER TWO

2

What was the first full-length Disney movie?

Disney's *Snow White* was a huge hit.

Snow White and the Seven Dwarfs in 1937. It was the first animated feature film made in America. It was over an hour long. Some thought this was too long for a cartoon. They were wrong. Both children and adults loved it! Today, Disney is known for its **blockbuster** movies.

SNOW WHITE AND THE SEVEN DWARFS **(1937): FIRST FULL-LENGTH ANIMATED MOVIE IN AMERICA**

MARY POPPINS **(1964): FIRST FEATURE FILM TO USE BOTH ANIMATION AND LIVE ACTION**

THE JUNGLE BOOK **(1994): FIRST LIVE-ACTION REMAKE OF AN ANIMATED DISNEY MOVIE**

TOY STORY **(1995): FIRST FULLY COMPUTER-ANIMATED MOVIE**

FROZEN II **(2019): HIGHEST-GROSSING DISNEY ANIMATED MOVIE**

Could I make a Disney movie?

Sure! But not alone. It takes hundreds of people working together. Every Disney movie starts with a great idea. Some people write the story. Others find voices for the characters. Today, artists mainly use computers for animation. A full movie can take five years from start to finish! Would you stick it out?

STORY TO SCREEN

1. Storyboard
2. Concept art
3. 3-D modeling
4. Shading and animation
5. Record voices
6. Final effects and sound

Disney's animation studio is in Burbank, California.

Coco

How many Disney movies are there?

Monsters, Inc.

Finding Dory

Disney has more than 60 animated movies. And there are more than 300 live-action movies! Many movies **stream** on Disney+ and other **TV networks**. The Disney Channel even makes its own movies. Disney also owns other movie companies. Pixar is one of them. This company helped make *Toy Story*.

Frozen II

DID YOU KNOW?
Walt Disney won 32 Academy Awards. That's a record!

What's it like at a Disney theme park?

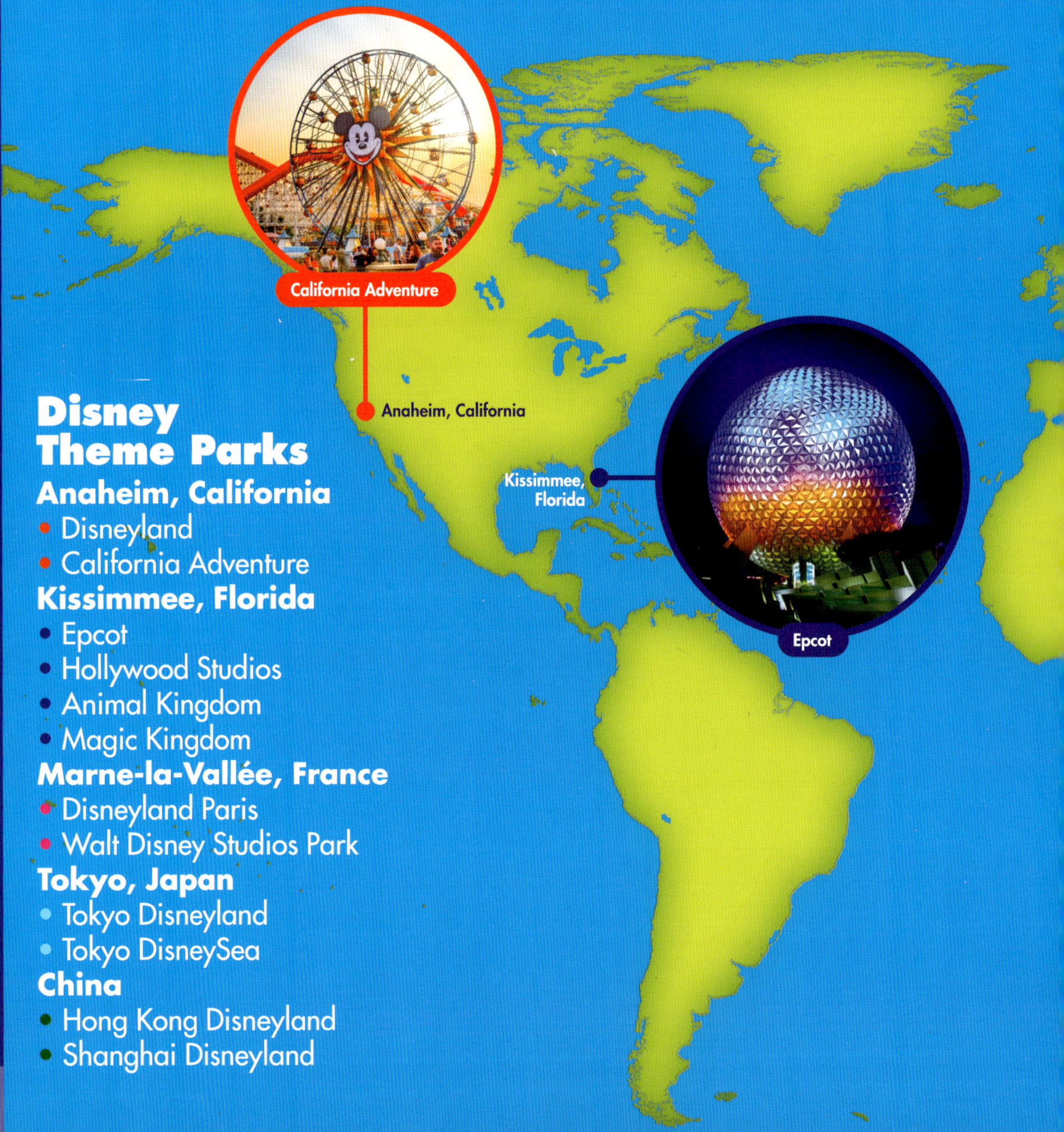

Disney Theme Parks

Anaheim, California
- Disneyland
- California Adventure

Kissimmee, Florida
- Epcot
- Hollywood Studios
- Animal Kingdom
- Magic Kingdom

Marne-la-Vallée, France
- Disneyland Paris
- Walt Disney Studios Park

Tokyo, Japan
- Tokyo Disneyland
- Tokyo DisneySea

China
- Hong Kong Disneyland
- Shanghai Disneyland

It can feel magical. The buildings and streets look like Disney movies. You can meet your favorite characters. There are rides, parades, and music. Every night, fireworks blast off behind the giant castle. There are 12 Disney parks around the world. Each is different from the rest.

Why do some Disney voices sound familiar?

It's probably someone famous. Many Disney characters have **celebrity** voices. It started with the big, blue Genie from *Aladdin*. He was voiced by actor Robin Williams. Early characters had unknown **voice actors**. But Genie's magic words changed movies forever. Which celebrity voices your favorite character?

Williams made up a lot of his own lines for Genie.

Who is the most famous Disney character?

Mickey is part of Disney's brand.

Almost everyone knows Mickey Mouse. He might not be your favorite. But he's been around the longest. Since 1928, Mickey has starred in more than 100 Disney movies and shorts. His look has changed over the years. But his round, black ears are a well-known Disney symbol.

Walt Disney voiced Mickey for 20 years.

DID YOU KNOW?
Mickey has a star on the Hollywood Walk of Fame.

Does Disney really use magic?

It sure seems that way! After all, it's called "the magical world of Disney." The real magic is the story. Disney tells stories that people of all ages love. The way each story touches their hearts feels magical. That's the gift of storytelling. It is the secret to Disney's big success.

Fireworks go off at Magic Kingdom in Florida.

STAY CURIOUS!

ASK MORE QUESTIONS

Where did Walt Disney grow up?

How many Disney short films are there?

Try a BIG QUESTION: How can I make an animated movie on my computer?

SEARCH FOR ANSWERS

Search the library catalog or the Internet.
A librarian, teacher, or parent can help you.

Using Keywords
Find the looking glass.

Keywords are the most important words in your question.

If you want to know about:

- Walt Disney's life, type: WALT DISNEY BIOGRAPHY
- Disney short movies, type: DISNEY SHORT FILMS

LEARN MORE

FIND GOOD SOURCES

Are the sources reliable?
Some sources are better than others. An adult can help you. Here are some good, safe sources.

Books

Disney
by Emma Huddleston, 2020.

Walt Disney
by Alicia Klepeis, 2022.

Internet Sites

Disney Now
https://disneynow.com/
Disney NOW is an interactive website with games, shows, and featured movies.

TED-ed: Make your own cartoon!
https://ed.ted.com/best_of_web/VxMuMORk
TED-ed is a non-profit educational site with videos on many topics.

Every effort has been made to ensure that these websites are appropriate for children. However, because of the nature of the Internet, it is impossible to guarantee that these sites will remain active indefinitely or that their contents will not be altered.

SHARE AND TAKE ACTION

Vote for your favorite Disney characters.
Include your family, friends, or classmates. Which character got the most votes?

Make a cartoon.
Work with friends to write a story, make drawings, and voice the characters.

Build a theme park in your yard!
Choose an idea, such as the ocean, a jungle, or your favorite story. Make activities, rides, and games that match your theme.

GLOSSARY

animation A type of movie or TV show made with cartoon drawings.

blockbuster Something that is very successful.

brand A group of products made or owned by the same company.

celebrity A famous person such as a movie star or pro athlete.

entertainment Activities people do for fun.

film To use a camera to record an action.

stream To send out a video using the internet for others to watch.

TV network A group of radio or TV stations that air the same type of programs.

theme park A large park with rides, activities, restaurants, and buildings that are all based on the same theme, or idea.

voice actor A person whose job is to provide the voice for a cartoon character.

INDEX

About the Author

Rachel Grack has been editing and writing children's books since 1999. She lives on a small ranch in southern Arizona. As a lover of stories, Disney is close to her heart.